KINGS LANDING

A LIVING HISTORY COLOURGUIDE

GEORGE PEABODY

PHOTOGRAPHY BY H.A. EISELT

FORMAC PUBLISHING COMPANY LIMITED
HALIFAX

Making rolls in the Ingraham kitchen

A village child enjoys the bounty of a country garden

Formac Publishing Company Limited acknowledges the
support of the Canada Council for the Arts for our publishing program. We acknowledge the support of the
Department of Canadian Heritage and the Nova Scotia
Department of Education and Culture in the development of writing and publishing in Canada.

Formac Publishing Company Limited
5502 Atlantic Street
Halifax, Nova Scotia
B3H 1G4

www.formac.ca

Canadian Cataloguing in Publication Data

Peabody, George.

Kings Landing.

(Living history colourguide)

ISBN 0-88780-398-9

1. Kings Landing Historical Settlement (N.B.) –
Guidebooks.
I. Eiselt, Horst A., 1950- II. Title. III. Series.
FC2465.K5P43 1997   971.5'51   C97-950010-9
F1042.8.P43 1997

Printed and bound in Canada.

Horsepower at work

Credits and Acknowledgements

The research and writing of this book would have been impossible without the cooperation of Darrell Butler, Kings Landing's Chief Curator, who gave generously of his time, sharing both his knowledge of and his enthusiasm for 19th century New Brunswick. I am also appreciative of the assistance of the staff of Woodstock's L.P. Fisher Library, whose Raymond Room contains a trove of material pertinent to the history of the region.

My greatest debt, as with any writer of history, is owed to my predecessors, the historians — professional and amateur — who have compiled and recorded, interpreted and analyzed, preserved and published the history of New Brunswick. The work of Peter Fisher, W.T. Baird, W.O. Raymond, Esther Clark Wright, Charlotte Gourlay Robinson, Elspeth Tulloch, Graeme Wynn, D.G. Bell, Scott W. See, and many others has prepared the ground. A further credit must go to those who have written with no thought of publication: the diarists and letter writers whose records of every-day family life are so valuable to our understanding of the past, and to the archivists who have preserved these documents.

Finally, I am indebted to my forebears, the Peabodys, Bedells, Bells, Stevensons, Bulls, Dibblees, and Carmans whose family cultures valued history and passed that value on.

CONTENTS

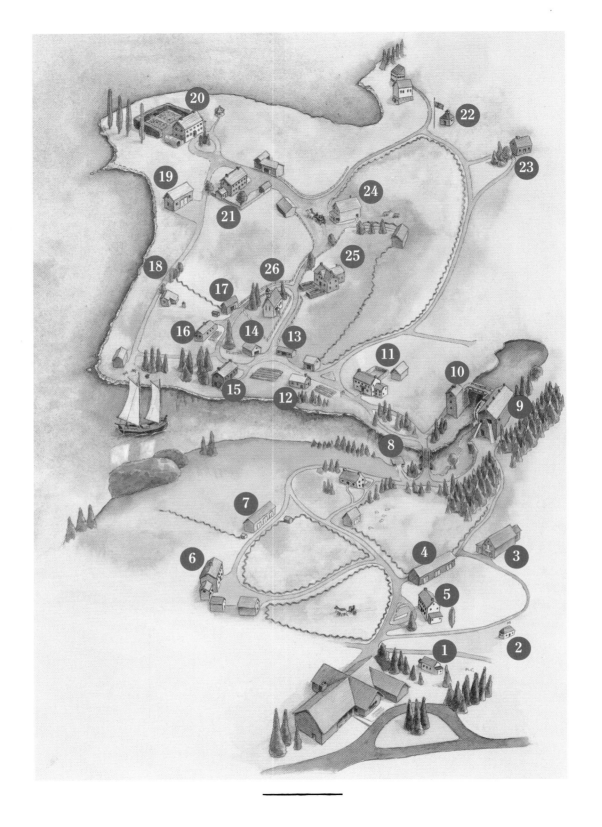

MAP LEGEND

1. The Agricultural Hall
2. The Printing Office
3. C.B. Ross Sash and Door Factory
4. The Carpenter Shop in the Red Barn
5. The Hagerman House
6. The Joslin Farm
7. The Jones House
8. The Brunswick Lion
9. The Sawmill
10. The Grist Mill
11. The Kings Head Inn
12. The Lint House
13. The Blacksmith Shop
14. The Ox Barn
15. The Long House
16. The Heustis House
17. The Cooper Shop
18. The Fisher House
19. The Ingraham Barn
20. The Ingraham House
21. The Morehouse House
22. The Parish School
23. The Killeen Cabin
24. The Grant Store
25. The Perley House
26. St. Mark's Church

PREFACE

Kings Landing Historical Settlement began as an off-shoot of one of the biggest hydro-electric projects in New Brunswick's history and as a major focus of New Brunswick's celebration of our nation's centennial in 1967. In the mid-1960s it was hoped that it would help to preserve New Brunswick's fast changing rural landscape and encourage the tourism industry by attracting people to our province.

As the settlement took shape, it soon became evident that Kings Landing would become much more. The people of New Brunswick, in the euphoria of Canada's Centennial celebration, opened their hearts, their stories, and their attic treasures to Kings Landing. As farm houses, mills, and workshops were meticulously restored, people were trained to bring the work of their ancestors back to life. Wood stoves that had not felt a cooking pot in ages were fired up and brought back to

life. Farm equipment was rebuilt and harnessed to horses again. Oxen, long out of use in New Brunswick, were trained to the yoke and the rattle of lumbering carts was

you to experience.

There is commitment to Kings Landing. From the historians and curators who ensure that it is a faithful recreation of New Brunswick's past, to the gift shop staff, restaurant staff, and the workers in our many homes, shops, and mills, that the visitors' experience will be the very best it can be. This commitment comes from a deep felt pride in our past and Kings Landing. This is part of the magic of Kings Landing.

Darrell N. Butler,
Chief Curator,
Kings Landing.

heard again on our roads. The stream was dammed and the water harnessed to saw wood and to grind grain. Gardens were tilled and planted with vegetables that had not been planted in decades. Animals were bred back to the old breeds of farm animals. Kings Landing became a great stage in which our past came to life.

There is a magic to Kings Landing. Visitors leave the present in the parking lot and our Visitor Reception Center. They stroll through Kings Landing and experience the past in every sense. They hear the cattle in the fields, the loon in the cove, and children playing in the school yard. They smell the kerosene of the oil lamps, the apple pie fresh from the bake oven, and the farm roses in the warm summer rain. They can reach out and touch the past at every turn, feel the sway of a farm wagon over the country roads, and run their hands over the hundred year old rails of our snake rail fences. There are the tastes of freshly grown vegetables, warm pies, and freshly squeezed lemonade. Our history is alive for

A VISIT TO KINGS LANDING

Kings Landing, located just off the Trans-Canada Highway 37 kilometres west of Fredericton, is a special sort of museum, a place where 19th century New Brunswick comes to life. A visit here is a feast for all five senses, from the ring of the blacksmith's hammer to the feel of the wooden stall smoothed by the necks of oxen; the aroma of a rhubarb pie fresh from the oven of a wood-fired cooking range, and the taste of venison in the dining room of the King's Head Inn. Every bend in a path offers a new vista; every room displays treasures.

A team of workhorses hauls the wagon type known as a "sloven" to transport visitors within the Settlement

The modern Visitor Centre at the entrance offers an introduction to the Village. Here, permanent displays provide visitors with background context for the Kings Landing they are about to experience. In the Centre's River Heritage Gallery, exhibitions change three times a season. The gift shop contains books and fine work from New Brunswick artists and artisans. A licensed restaurant in the Centre offers contemporary, popularly priced meals.

Stepping out of the Visitor Centre and into Kings Landing is a movement in space and in time. Pause for a moment here on the threshold of the village and look out over the fields and trees and buildings of the community. Life in the 19th century is waiting.

Piecing a quilt — the 19th century had no time for idle hands

Visiting cousins chat on a traditional split cedar rail fence

Plan on at least half a day at Kings Landing; most visits to the site are four to five hours, and a full day can easily slip by while you are experiencing 19th century life. On a trip back in time to an age where time is measured in days and seasons, you may find yourself adapting to the rhythms of a slower-paced way of life.

Visiting Kings Landing means walking. The village covers approximately 90 acres. As with many of the 19th century's rural communities, its buildings are spread along a network of roads and paths. It is approximately 1.2 kilometres from the entrance to the other side of the settlement. The walking is not rough, but the 19th century is underfoot as well as around you: don't expect asphalt or concrete, and do wear comfortable walking shoes.

You may break your walk with a ride: wagons drawn by teams of workhorses carry visitors from the entrance to the centre of the village and back, and are popular with young and old alike. Where possible, historic buildings have been made accessible to wheelchairs.

Kings Landing is open to visitors daily from 10 a.m. to 5 p.m. between June 1 and Thanksgiving. In addition, the village offers a range of theme and school programs, evening workshops in such 19th century skills as open-hearth cooking, and special events such as the annual fall agricultural fair. Guided tours are available with advance reservation for groups of 20 or more.

With more than 120 costumed interpreters, live theatrical performances twice a day, strolling musicians, and the busy daily

Harvest bounty

Mother and child

life of a 19th century agricultural village, Kings Landing is a very special sort of museum.

Amenities on site include restrooms at the Visitor Centre, the King's Head Inn, and the Prince William Ice Cream Parlour. There are picnic tables at the ice cream parlour and the inn.

The King's Head provides an authentic 19th century dining experience, a taste of the 1800's with a menu featuring pheasant, venison and rabbit. Costumed servers, candlelight and music highlight evening programs at the Inn.

After a visit to Kings Landing, with five senses replete, the visitor may develop a sixth: a sense of better understanding and appreciation for the lives of our ancestors.

THE LOYALISTS AND 19TH CENTURY NEW BRUNSWICK

Kings Landing Historical Settlement re-creates a 19th century New Brunswick village, a community founded by

On the way to school

A black powder shot

the Loyalists and largely peopled by their descendants.

Who were the Loyalists? There is a Loyalist reality and a Loyalist myth.

became bitter, and extreme pressure was often exerted to force the reluctant to declare themselves openly. Later accounts by Loyalists tell of mobs of "patriotic" neighbours harassing and terrorizing those they knew or suspected of supporting the Crown. When dissent broke into open war, loyal Americans formed regiments to fight for their King and for their homes. They were among the most active and the most successful fighters for the Crown, and were often highly critical of the shortcomings of the British politicians and military strategists.

When the war was lost, the loyal Americans lost the most. Already the war had uprooted and driven many of them from their homes, concentrating their numbers in areas under British control, particularly in and near New York. At war's end, unable to return to properties that had been seized by hostile former neighbours, they sought refuge elsewhere under the Crown. In all, some 80,000 men, women and children left their old homes in the new United States; 15,000 of them arrived in what became New Brunswick in fleets of refugee ships between 1783 and 1784.

The reality is that the Loyalists were refugees, former residents of Britain's 13 American colonies who had supported the losing side. It is sometimes thought today that the revolutionary war of independance which racked the American colonies between 1775 and 1783 was a simple struggle between an autocratic king and democratic colonists, red-coated British soldiers fighting on one side, united citizen armies on the other.

The truth is that there were all shades of opinion among Americans, from the most radical advocates of independence, to rock-steady supporters of the established order. Divisions in communities and even in families

Here, they surveyed and built the city of Saint John, and founded towns and villages along the Fundy coast. Most of them moved inland to establish farms on land they had been granted in the river valleys, especially the St. John River Valley.

New Brunswick's Loyalists were a diverse group: farmers, labourers, tradesmen and craftsmen, widows, sailors, merchants, lawyers and officials, whose only certain common characteristic was their loyalty to the Crown. They included servants, some of whom were Black and may have been slaves cloaked under a euphemism. There were also free Black Loyalists who had gained their freedom by supporting the King.

For almost everyone in the first generation of Loyalists, establishing themselves in New Brunswick was a struggle. Many had been able to salvage a little from their lives in New England, New York or Virginia. Others had lost almost all they possessed when their "world turned upside down," and some no doubt had little enough to begin with, arriving destitute.

Stark images remain of the hardship of the first winters in New Brunswick: boards heated near the open fire and pressed against the children for warmth when families had no bedding, deep snow in November before even crude huts had been completed for shelter, heroic midwinter journeys on foot through snow and intense cold to bring back flour to feed a starving family.

The Loyalists did not suffer in silence. Having lost much because of their support of the Crown, they felt entitled to some support from the Crown, and they petitioned it vigorously for assistance and compensation for their losses. Emergency assistance was provided. "We all had rations given us by the government, flour, butter and pork. Tools were given to the men also," recorded the young Hannah Ingraham, whose home in later life is one of the houses now at Kings Landing.

Family kin learning the art of blacksmithing

Despite the aid, most Loyalist families endured hard times starting over in a new country. Even the less well off had lived in established communities before the war, and most had been accustomed to a measure of security and domestic comfort. Rebuilding was a daunting task.

The primary benefits the Crown provided to its loyal supporters in New Brunswick consisted of land grants. Urban lots in the new city of Saint John were distributed by lottery, though there was suspicion at the time that the more influential Loyalists got special treatment and more desirable locations.

Rural land grants were allotted to heads of families, with the size of the grant determined by status. Most grants were taken up, if not always by the original grantees, and the Loyalists settled in to rebuild their lives. The first years were the hardest, and by the early 19th century most Loyalist families were settled on farms which provided a level of security and even comfort. Many had built back up to the level they or their parents had enjoyed before the war.

The principal Loyalist myth depicts the Loyalists as an elite, the land-owning gentry, the merchant and official class of Colonial America, overthrown and perhaps impoverished by the forces of revolution, but a sort of aristocracy still.

Like all myths, it contains an element of truth. Among the thousands of Loyalists who came to New Brunswick could be found individuals who fit the image: men who had raised colonial regiments for the King, who had owned plantations in Virginia, or had held high official posts in the colonial governments. Some of them at least, knew the sort of New Brunswick they wished to create. It would have, as Edward Winslow wrote to Ward Chipman, "the most Gentlemanlike" constitution "on Earth." Their attempts to create this antithesis to democracy faced many obstacles, not the least of which was the attitude of their fellow Loyalists, who

View of Morehouse and Ingraham Houses

were often uncooperative and frequently antagonistic. Loyal to the Crown they might be, but not necessarily passively obedient to the servants of the Crown. Many felt little loyalty and less respect for those fellow refugees who considered themselves their "social betters" and expected special privileges on that account.

Despite the opposition, the Loyalist elite managed to control New Brunswick's government for more than a generation, and drew useful incomes from the salaries and perquisites which attended public office in the late 18th and early 19th centuries. But they were unable to establish the great landed estates they had dreamed of carving from the New Brunswick forests, and their power and influence waned as the 19th century unfolded.

The myth, however, gathered strength even as the power of the Loyalist elite was being eroded by the huge changes taking place in 19th century New Brunswick. The progress of these changes may be charted through the buildings and artifacts of Kings Landing.

Few of the first Loyalist buildings survive in New Brunswick. The oldest one at Kings Landing is a curiosity: an elegant octagonal privy built in the 1790's for The Barony, the large country estate of John Saunders in

Dumfries parish. Perhaps it is an appropriate memorial to the pretensions of the Loyalist elite.

A prominent early New Brunswick Loyalist, who bridged the generation of those who came as adults and the generation of those born in the province, was Peter Fisher, who was one year old when his parents reached Fredericton. At Kings Landing he is associated with the very early 19th century saltbox-style Fisher House, which he owned and where he may have lived briefly as a young man. Fisher is remembered as New Brunswick's first historian for his 1825 *Sketches of New Brunswick Containing an Account of the First Settlement of the Province*. He became a prosperous Fredericton merchant.

Several Kings Landing houses are among those built by first generation Loyalists or their children as replacements for original dwellings once their improving fortunes permitted. Perhaps the most interesting of these are the Morehouse House of 1812, and the stone Jones House of about 1828.

The dwellings in 19th century villages in the St. John River Valley were not exclusively built and occupied by Loyalists and their descendants, and neither were those of Kings Landing. Soon after the turn of the century, immigrants, principally from the British Isles, began to arrive in some numbers. Between 1810 and 1840, the population of New Brunswick grew dramatically. Most immigrants came seeking opportunity in a new country where land was readily available and wages were high. They arrived with substantial personal belongings, skills in established trades to support themselves, and capital to invest. Others, especially those fleeing poverty in Ireland, arrived with little more than the clothes on their backs, and faced struggles as hard as any endured by their Loyalist predecessors to create new beginnings for their families. The simple Killeen Cabin, set back from the river in the backwoods of Kings Landing, is typical of the first homes they built.

As well as farms, the St. John River Valley provided numerous suitable sites for water-powered mills on tributary streams: saw-mills to increase the value and utility of trees cut from the forest, and grist mills to grind flour from the grain grown on the farms. Kings Landing demonstrates a sawmill of about 1830, and a grist mill of 1885.

Mills were not the only rural industries. Almost every farming community had a blacksmith, who shod horses and oxen and crafted a wide range of everyday objects and tools from iron and steel. Many communities provided work for a fine carpenter builder, like James Mitchell, whose skill is seen in several Kings Landing houses. Wheelwrights built the carts and wagons. Coopers supplied casks and barrels. Small tanneries produced leather, and fulling and carding mills processed wool.

By mid-century, larger industries were developing, such as carriage and sleigh factories, foundries, manufacturers of farm equipment, cheese factories, and sash and door factories. Transportation improved: steamboats carried passengers and freight seasonally on the St. John River from the Reversing Falls to Grand Falls, roads were better built and better maintained, and by the final quarter of the century railways had begun to draw custom away from both roads and river.

Throughout the 19th century, New Brunswick enjoyed an increasing population and an expanding economy. The confidence of the times is reflected in such houses at Kings Landing as the Ingraham House, with its impressive hedged garden, the Hagerman House, and the quintessentially Victorian Perley House.

At work at the Saxony spinning wheel

Even more than in the houses, the prosperity may be seen in furnishings. Collections of fine furniture by Thomas Nisbet displayed in the Ingraham House, and by John Warren Moore in the Hagerman House, are evidence that 19th century New Brunswick produced some of the finest furniture ever built in Canada.

Kings Landing is much more than its buildings and artifacts and the stories of the families who possessed them. It is a living history, a working community animated by contemporary New Brunswickers in authentic costumes of the 19th century carrying out the daily tasks in household and farm, shop and mill, who bring the community alive. In the vivid 19th century setting of buildings, fields and gardens, the farmers and farm wives, spinsters and bachelors and children illustrate the fascinating history of the everyday life of our ancestors.

Traditional carriage

THE AGRICULTURAL HALL

The Agricultural Hall, a late 19th century building used for visitor orientation and special displays

Our tour of Kings Landing begins at the small Agricultural Hall building on the right as you enter the Settlement. A typical late 19th century rural building, the Hall holds orientation exhibits for visitors.

For the Loyalists, farming meant survival in their new home. No matter what their backgrounds — many had been tradesmen or merchants in colonial America — all those who took up land grants in rural New Brunswick became farmers from necessity. The first generation laboured to clear land and grow the crops which fed the family; in good years there might be a surplus for sale, but family survival was the aim.

As farms became better established, farmers became

Examining the crop

more concerned with improving agriculture. Different varieties of grains and vegetables were introduced and evaluated, purebred livestock began to replace the old mixed breeds, and the commercial aspect of farming became more important.

Accompanying and assisting with the improvements in agriculture were the local, county and provincial agricultural societies established in the first half of the 19th century. The societies grew to have many practical and social functions. They imported better seed varieties and new animal breeds; they provided a forum for farmers to meet and exchange information; they presented talks and lectures, and they sponsored fairs and stock shows, exhibitions and competitions.

Ox teams powered many farms

The fall auction at the Agricultural Hall

Setting up for a corn boil

THE PRINTING OFFICE

Reconstruction of a typical late 19th century "jobbing" printer's shop

United States or Upper Canada, ordered by the printer from a specialty supplier in Toronto or Montreal and shipped by the railways, the printing presses are emblems of the 19th century Age of Progress.

Much of the equipment remained in use until well into the 20th century and was acquired by Kings Landing from print shops in St. Andrews, St. Stephen and other New

Standards of education improved and the level of literacy rose throughout New Brunswick during the second half of the 19th century. Newspapers and journals proliferated in the towns, and even in small communities there was an increasing demand for printed products. Posters for the agricultural society, tickets for balls, bills, advertising flyers and suchlike day-to-day printing jobs were the mainstay of the small "jobbing printers" shops which grew up to meet local needs.

The Printing Office at Kings Landing is a reconstruction of a typical jobber's shop of the 1890's. The type cabinets, printer's stone, paper cutter and foot powered platen presses are the tools of the 19th century printer's trade. Manufactured in Europe, the

A specialized cabinet for storing lead type

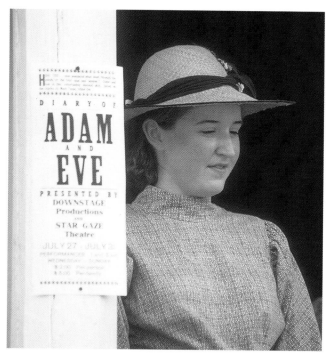

Brunswick communities. The layout of the building is based on St. Andrews' Beacon Printing Office, which also provided the front doors. Samples of the printer's trade are displayed on the counter.

A playbill and a theatre-goer

The printer's apprentice — sometimes called the "printer's devil" — at work on the press

A row of platen presses await work

THE C.B. ROSS SASH AND DOOR FACTORY

The C.B. Ross Sash and Door Factory; the 2nd floor entry was handy for moving materials in and out

Charles Balfour Ross was a determined man. Born in Blackville on the Miramichi in 1878, he decided as a youth that he wanted to be a carpenter. At the age of 16, he was sufficiently assured and accomplished that, encouraged by his father, he accepted his first contract; to build a house for a local resident. This early experience may have prompted him to set a slightly different direction for his future: soon after, he apprenticed himself to the largest sash and door factory in Nova Scotia where he worked for a full seven year term.

Ross realized that the technology of house building had changed. Gone were the days when carpenters like James Mitchell had used their block planes to carefully shape trim and had made their doors and windows by hand. The 19th century was the Age of Machinery, and by its close, steam-powered moulders, tenon machines, band saws and other equipment had sped up and standardized the production of building trim, doors and windows. Sash and door factories, large and small, were found in many communities.

The tool box was an invaluable resource

When young C.B. Ross first returned to Blackville from

Detail of moulding machine

his Nova Scotia apprenticeship, he worked for and later purchased a local sash, door and bob-sled factory. He improved the factory with additional machinery and a larger steam engine for power, and ran it as part of a larger building contract business.

One story about Ross indicates how house building had changed by the early 20th century. He became locally famous for building a two storey house, complete, in only two weeks by pre-cutting all the parts in his factory and shipping them to the site organized on a railway flatcar in the order in which they would be needed.

As with the printing business, the equipment in the Ross factory demonstrates links with the "global economy" of the time: it was manufactured elsewhere, perhaps ordered from catalogues and shipped by rail.

The Ross factory continued under C.B., and later his son, until it closed in 1950. All the equipment was preserved by the family and eventually donated to Kings Landing. The present C.B. Ross Sash and Door Factory displays this equipment in a working replica of his early 20th century factory.

Sled factory

THE CARPENTER SHOP IN THE RED BARN

Barns were important and prominent features of the 19th century rural landscape. They were tall imposing buildings designed to store hay and straw in their upper lofts and house animals and farm equipment below. The Red Barn, an unusually long structure, has been restored to its original appearance at a time when it housed a large number of cattle and sheep.

At Kings Landing, one end of the barn has been adapted as an 1870 woodworking shop, where the traditional trades of carpentry and wheelwrighting are brought back to life for visitors. Here the carpenter uses hand tools to meet the woodworking needs of the community, from mouldings and trim to coffins. The elaborate hearse stored here — as it might well have been kept in the carpenter's shop until needed — is a reminder of the role of death in 19th century society.

Carpentry, of course, continues today as a skilled trade. But the art of the wheelwright, crucial in the 19th century, has all but vanished. In the old horse-powered rural economy, the craftsman who made the wheels for wagons, carts and carriages was one of the most respected and best paid of any of the specialists. Constructed from different types of wood — each wheel component from hub to felloes to spokes had its particular preferred

The long red barn contains the carpenter's and wheelwright's shops

wood — shaped to precision, assembled and held in place by the tension of its components secured by the iron rim shrunk onto it, each wheel was a work of art.

Shaving a spoke

In a small 19th century village, the carpenter made the simple coffins and sometimes also kept the hearse — here, with its winter runners attached

THE HAGERMAN HOUSE

The Neo-Classic Hagerman House

When John Hagerman Jr., farmer, landowner, Captain in the York County Militia, felt able to afford a new house on his Bear Island property in the early 1830's, he chose the Neo-Classical style fashionable then. He followed a local building tradition, framing his house with hand-hewn timbers in a modified post and beam style. For the interior finish and detail work, Hagerman commissioned the respected local carpenter James Mitchell, a Scottish immigrant whose interior detailing may be seen in several Kings Landing houses.

Unfortunately, John Hagerman did not enjoy his new house for long because he died in 1838. Even more unfortunate for his widow and seven children, he left no will, touching off legal complications which entangled the property for 25 years.

But this black legal cloud held a silver lining for historians as well as for lawyers; Hagerman's intestacy resulted in the compilation of a detailed valuation of all his assets. The lists give some insight into relative values at the time; Hagerman's four oxen were worth as much as all his household furniture; his one horse had nearly twice the value of his farming equipment.

Perhaps due in part to the legal situation, two of Hagerman's sons and their wives and children jointly occupied the house until 1863. The census of 1851 shows 13 people living there. But joint occupancy by extended families was a common household pattern in the 19th century. Particularly in rural communities, the family and the home were the basis of social and economic life, and it was taken for granted that old and young alike had their contributions to make.

Now restored to its 1870 appearance, the Hagerman House reflects the presence of a young Victorian family. In its present form, the house also serves another purpose of Kings Landing: the display of fine furniture from New

"Lady's" and "Gentleman's" chairs made by New Brunswick furniture maker John Warren Moore whose work is featured in the Hagerman House

Keeping the birds from the garden — sometimes "bird-scaring" was one of the first jobs for farm children rather than relegated to a scarecrow

The elegant dining room, reserved, in the Victorian custom, for special occasions

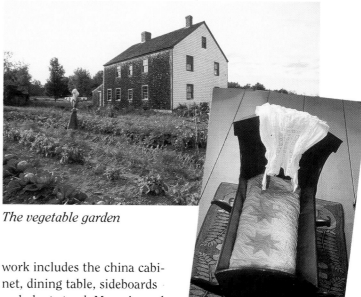

The vegetable garden

A hooded cradle in the parents' room

A mahogany rocker in the parents' room

Brunswick's 19th century craftsmen. In particular, the Hagerman House showcases pieces by St. Stephen cabinetmaker John Warren Moore, who worked from 1833 to 1883. As with the surviving work of other 19th century New Brunswick furniture makers, Moore's work reflects a keen awareness of styles and materials in vogue elsewhere.

We know somewhat more about Moore's life than about many of his contemporaries. His wife Louisa was a prolific and highly literate letter writer, and many of her letters have survived. She describes visits to Boston and New York, writes to and of relatives who have moved to England and the United States, and describes the daily life of a middle class Victorian household. Ease of travel and speed of communications improved throughout the century; even rural parts of New Brunswick participated in the complex patterns of the time.

In the Hagerman dining room — like most Victorian dining rooms, not a room for everyday use — Moore's

work includes the china cabinet, dining table, sideboards and plant stand. Moore's work also dominates in the parlour, where the "Lady's" and "Gentleman's" chairs, with their graceful cabriole legs, and the large secretary desk, with Gothic-arched glass doors resembling church windows, are of particular interest.

The upper rooms in the Hagerman House indicate the presence of three generations. Moore's work fills the parents' bedroom and the "granny" room. In the girl's room, the doll's chest of drawers and bed were made by Moore's son Harry.

In the boy's bedroom, a print of a locomotive decorates a wall. Trains were no longer a novelty in the New Brunswick of 1870, although railways had yet to make their appearance in this part of the St. John River Valley. J.W. Moore himself was an early investor in the Saint Andrews and Quebec Railway Company, an enterprise with ambitions that ran far in advance of its ability to lay track. Small investors like Moore saw no return on their money, nor, as his wife Louisa complained in a letter some years after, even "the least privilege, a pass over the road, etc., while the moneyed men who gave five, ten, or fifteen thousand, have passed over the road with all their families ever since".

THE JOSLIN FARM

The Joslin Farm is typical of the agriculture practised on well-established New Brunswick farms in the middle years of the 19th century. By 1860, the Joslins were a prosperous farming family, headed by William Cook Joslin, then 66 years old and the son of the Loyalist who built the house and founded the farm. Also living in the house and working on the farm at the time of the 1861 census were two of Joslin's sons, his daughter, a 14-year-old farm labourer and two servants, one of whom was William McCulyer, a 21-year-old Black man.

The house in which they lived is a good example of how dwellings evolved. The main section was built in the 1790's. Fifty years later, another generation added the wing, the carriage shed, and the Classic Revival doorway with its sidelights. The renovations reflected increasing prosperity; the Joslins owned and operated a sawmill as well as their farm.

Increasing prosperity and changing times are also evident in some of the furnishings. The kitchen has an iron cooking stove, a New Brunswicker model manufactured by the Harris and Allen foundry. Kerosene lamps were also used, which was a major advance over the tallow candles and rushlights of previous generations.

Like all working farms, the Joslin Farm includes a number of outbuildings: the horse barn, stable, piggery, stock barn and sheds. Outbuildings were important for storage as well as for seasonal shelter for farm animals.

At the beginning of the 19th century, most farm animals in New Brunswick were mixed breeds, all-purpose creatures the predominant characteristic of which was hardiness, the ability to survive by foraging when other food was scanty, as it often was when farms were still being cut

The Joslin Farm with its house and range of outbuildings is a typical 19th century working farm

The pantry offers a fine display of crockery

6

China on display

The barns of the late 19th and early 20th century were often works of rural craft and art

and burned out of the forest. As farms became established, however, attention shifted from survival to the improvement of breeds. Pure-bred stock was imported and selective breeding programs undertaken.

The variety and range of animals raised on 19th century farms is impressive. Few farmers

A fanning mill for cleaning grain

Home Manufacturing and Commerce noted in 1854, "The Alligator breed [was] disappearing slowly, and the Hampshire, Chinese and Berkshires taking their place."

At the end of the 20th century, agricultural specialization has intensified enormously, and many of the common "improved" breeds of the 19th century have become rare "heritage" breeds. Some of these have found a home on the Joslin Farm at Kings Landing.

A rosewood-cased melodeon made in Massachusetts in 1851

were specialists: they kept oxen and horses for power, and raised sheep, pigs, cattle and chickens. Many also raised ducks, geese and turkeys. By 1872, at least 18 different breeds of chicken — from Speckled Dorkings to Bramba Pootra Fowls — were being raised on New Brunswick farms, as well as five breeds of duck and three of geese. The original pigs were reminiscent of the pigs in medieval paintings. They were black, hairy, long-snouted ridgebacks, known in 18th century North America as alligator pigs. By the middle of the 19th century, as the Journal of the New Brunswick Society for the Encouragement of Agriculture,

THE JONES HOUSE

Stone houses are uncommon in rural New Brunswick. But Thomas Jones was not a common man in any sense of the term. Family legend records that he was in the midst of building his fine new stone house when word came that his wife had just given birth to his first-born son. Following his own sense of priorities, Thomas Jones continued to lay stone, finishing the upstairs window on which he was working before going to see his wife and new-born son. That son, named Simeon after his grandfather, left the farm as a young man, moving to Saint John where he managed and later owned a brewery, established a bank and became a city councillor and eventually mayor. In Saint John, he too built a stone house.

Thomas Jones came from a prosperous Loyalist family. His father, Simeon, held a position in the law courts of colonial New Hampshire, and his grandfather, Elisha Jones, a wealthy landowner and militia commander, was a member of the Tory elite of Massachusetts.

The small "back" staircase was for work, not show

Dry stone retaining walls flank the path to the front door of the 1820 Jones House

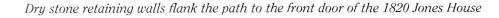

Upstairs stove

Built into a sidehill site, the Jones House is two storeys in front but only one above ground at the back

In 1827, Thomas Jones married Jane Caverhill, the daughter of a Scottish doctor and farmer who had immigrated to New Brunswick in 1820. Together, they founded a household representative of the better-off Loyalist families of the time.

The Jones House, with its solid stone construction, classical proportions and rich interior trim, suggests the status of its owners: Thomas Jones was a Justice of the Peace, later a Magistrate, Captain and then Paymaster in the Militia, and an Anglican Church warden. Yet it also displays the reality of a working farmhouse, with its milk room and storage cellar. And the stone walls, though thick, are not warm: some rooms have their plaster applied directly to the stone; the others have only lath and plaster with little insulative value. In cold winter weather, the large fireplaces struggled to bring warmth to the elegant rooms.

The furnishings in the Jones House reflect the Jones family's experience in Colonial America. A pembroke table that belonged to Elisha Jones stands in a parlour corner; Simeon's pocket watch and the family Bible grace the master bedroom. The surveyor's chain in the study was used by Thomas to survey many of the farms in Prince William parish.

From the road past the Jones House, a path leads to Courser's Cove, the inlet where a dock connects community and river.

Gentlemen taking tea in the parlour

THE BRUNSWICK LION

Specialized "wooden boats" were built and used along the St. John River in the 19th century

Although the very name of Kings Landing Historical Settlement emphasizes the river, it is still easy to underestimate the practical importance of the St. John River in the day-to-day lives of the settlements which grew up on its banks in the 19th century. For the early settlers, the river was the transportation route: it brought them and all their worldly goods upstream to new homes, brought supplies up from the port, floated rafts of logs and lumber down to the port for export, and took their farm surplus — when they had any — to market. Compared with the rudimentary roads, the river, although occasionally hazardous, was quick and reliable.

In the 19th century, the river was lively with boats.

Riverside settlers rowed, poled, and paddled their canoes and boats up, down and across the river to visit their friends and relatives, attend church and do business. From freshet to freeze-up, commercial craft plied the river, laden tow boats — drawn by horses or oxen plodding along the bankside tow-path — making their slow progress up against the current. By mid-century, steamboats had begun to appear, a practical improvement and also an occasion for celebration. New Brunswick historian W.O. Raymond recalls that his father, "a member of the first Woodstock Band, in which he played a bass instrument called an Ophiclyde... went on an excursion in the steamer *Reindeer* up the St. John River to the

The main village road crosses the creek

were designed to draw little water because of the high rapids at the river's mouth, but were often so heavily laden that they sailed with the deck practically level with the water, with a crew of two or three scrambling about on the stacks of lumber.

In Saint John, the boats had to cope with the extreme tidal range of the Bay of Fundy. Boats well afloat at high tide were often aground on the mud flats at low tide. The woodboats were built with very low keels and had blocks or "bilge keels" underneath to keep them upright at low tide.

Nearly 300 woodboats were built along the banks of the river in the 1800's. The last known original woodboat survived until 1936, when it ran aground and sank.

The Brunswick Lion is a reconstructed woodboat, based on an original registered in Saint John in 1837. After detailed and meticulous research, the Lion was constructed by hand during the summer of 1975.

Grand Falls in the year 1847, being the first occasion on which a steamer had visited Grand Falls."

The most unique, but perhaps the most common 19th century vessels on the river were the woodboats. The design of these small schooners evolved from early boats used by the Loyalists, and by the 1830's they had become a special type built only in the St. John River Valley. While they would carry any paying cargo, the woodboat was designed to transport large quantities of planks, then known as "deals", from the sawmills of the Valley to buyers in Saint John, or even as far down the Atlantic coast as Boston. Planks were loaded in the hull and then laid in stacks across the deck. For maximum cargo space, the deck was wide and the forward mast placed as far into the bow as possible, giving the bow a round or snub-nosed appearance. The woodboats

The Brunswick Lion displays her ribs — 19th century woodboats had an average lifetime of less than 20 years

THE SAWMILL

The sawmill with its overshot waterwheel

The vertical saw blade moves slowly through a deal

New Brunswick's heart is the forest. More than 85 percent of the province is still classed as forest land. But even before the first Acadian settlers cleared farms in the 17th century, the harvest of New Brunswick's trees had begun. By the time the Loyalist refugees arrived in the St. John River Valley late in the 18th century, timbering and the timber trade were well established. The trade could be lucrative and highly competitive: in the 1770's, rival harvesting crews of Planters from the Maugerville settlement, and Scots previously based on the Miramichi conducted what was almost a small private war over the rights to cut the pines of the Nashwaak Valley.

Initially, the logs were exported unfinished for use as naval masts and spars. Later, logs might be shaped with axe or adze into square timbers, or even sawn into boards and planks with man-powered pit-saws. Before the beginning of the 19th century, increasing local demand for lumber prompted the establishment of sawmills. These water-powered sawmills, which the Loyalists and their descendants began to build on suitable creeks

Massive wooden gears transmit the power

32

and power the vertical sawblade.

In New Brunswick's climate, water-powered sawmills were seasonal operations, running from April or May until freeze-up in December. On some streams, low water might reduce or even halt sawing in dry summers. Most mills were run by families who farmed and timbered as well. Thus the sawmill was part of an overall business, sawing lumber from their own logs and custom sawing for others.

As the 19th century continued and New Brunswick's timber trade became larger and ever better organized, small water-powered sawmills lost out to the larger, more efficient and much faster steam-powered mills.

Local sawmills depended on the local blacksmith for iron work

and brooks, were usually small, one or two man operations. Like the Kings Landing sawmill, which is a reproduction of a typical 1830's mill, the early mills were powered by large waterwheels. Motion was transferred through huge wooden gears to move the log carriage

The mill and its image in the tranquil creek

THE GRIST MILL

Most early 19th century agriculture was based on grain. Loyalist farmers in the St. John River Valley, as historian Peter Fisher recorded in 1825, grew wheat, rye, oats, buckwheat, "Indian Corn or Maize," some barley and even millet. But without local grist mills to grind their crops of grain into flour and meal, farmers were at a great disadvantage, forced to ship their grain to distant markets and to buy imported flour for their own consumption. There were many suitable sites along the Valley, but mills were expensive to build and equip. Both individuals and groups of settlers frequently petitioned the Province for grants to assist in the construction of

A reconstruction of an 1880's grist mill

mills. Grants were often made, but even 40 years after Loyalist settlement began, New Brunswick imported more than 40,000 barrels of wheat flour. The province's farms and mills fell far short of meeting the needs of the overall population.

Even quite early in the century, some communities had sufficient mills for local competition. In 1803, Frederick Dibblee notes in his diary that from one local mill he "Brought the Flower of 6 Bushels of Wheat — wt. 273 lbs. Ten Pounds more than 6 Bushels Produced from Mr. Allen's mill." Many mills were seasonal operations, and Dibblee frequently notes that low water or cold weather kept the mills from grinding. And they were high risk businesses: many millers shared the experience of James Morris, who discovered early one January morning in 1828 that his two-year-old mill at Lake George "was on fire and before he could get to it, it was Entirely Burned to the ground," a total financial loss "he verily believe[d] would fall little short of £200."

By the later 19th century, local milling was on the decline. Western wheat, transportation improvements and changes in milling technology permitted the large mills of Central Canada to produce the more desirable white flour, gradually driving the local mills to specialize. Some switched to grinding for animal feed. Others, like the present Kings Landing mill, set their stones to

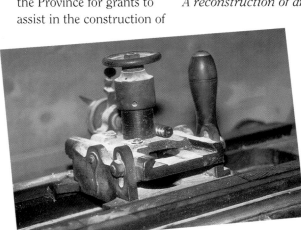

Grindstone sharpener

grind buckwheat.

Buckwheat had always been a favoured local crop, reliable in short growing seasons and capable of producing relatively large yields on marginal lands. A barrel of buckwheat flour was found in most farmhouse kitchens. The mill at Kings Landing is a typical 1885 operation. The building itself is a reconstruction of the Jeffries Mill, which once stood at Sussex Corner. The origins of this mill offer an interesting picture of early industrial

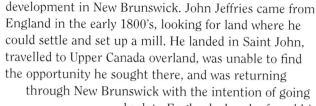

development in New Brunswick. John Jeffries came from England in the early 1800's, looking for land where he could settle and set up a mill. He landed in Saint John, travelled to Upper Canada overland, was unable to find the opportunity he sought there, and was returning through New Brunswick with the intention of going back to England when he found his spot at Sussex Corner. Here he built his first mill, importing the grindstones and milling equipment from England. Over the years, the mill was modernized, and a sawmill and carding mill were added to the operation. The mills remained in the Jeffries family for generations.

Mill machinery was often imported

Within the building, the Kings Landing grist mill uses equipment from the Jewett family mill at Mactaquac. It illustrates a typical late 19th century situation: an older mill which has recently been refurbished with new equipment. An efficient Laffel turbine has been set into the sluiceway in the basement to power the equipment throughout the mill. Buckwheat is delivered to the ground floor and carried by a grain elevator to the third floor. From there, it is gravity fed back to a smutter on the second floor which cleans the grain before it reaches the grindstones on the ground floor. After grinding, the flour is sifted through the bolter, and is then ready for use, perhaps to make the buckwheat pancakes which were a staple rural meal at the time.

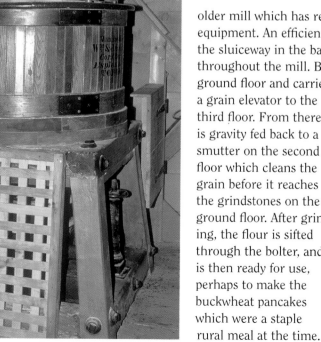

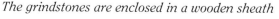

The grindstones are enclosed in a wooden sheath

THE KING'S HEAD INN

The King's Head Inn

The pub

Drink was also abundant — too much so, according to some opinion. From the 1820's on, temperance movements fought against the easy availability of alcohol at the province's inns and taverns. In the middle 1850's, the anti-drink lobby was strong enough to pass a prohibition act in the legislature. There was, however, a huge public outcry. A new election was called, and a new legislature emphatically ended prohibition six months after it had begun. It did not end the temperance movement, which waxed and waned in popularity and political influence throughout the Victorian Era, gradually establishing the social climate which produced the alcohol restrictions of the 20th century. Like other community organizations — the Masonic and Orange Lodges, and the Mechanics' Institutes — temperance societies had roles in community social life far beyond their ostensible purpose. Their meetings were social occasions, their members supported each other in a variety of ways, and they provided ready-made social frameworks for young men and women moving to new communities. By late in the century, they had begun to spawn temperance hotels as an alternative to the temptations of taverns.

When Isabella Lucy Bird, an Englishwoman travelling through New Brunswick in 1854, arrived at one rural inn, she found it "so full that my hostess said she could not give me a bed... and with considerable complacency she took me into a large, whitewashed, carpetless room, furnished with one chair, a small table, and my valise. She gave me two buffalo robes, and left me..."

Beds were sometimes scarce, and bedrooms frequently shared, in rural New Brunswick's 19th century inns, but food was abundant. "Everything to satisfy a hungry man is here," wrote W.T. Baird in his *Seventy Years of New Brunswick Life*. "Ham and eggs, fowl, venison of moose or deer (found within a hundred yards), pies, doughnuts, and the inevitable applesauce."

The tap room

Open for business

point between where you began and where you were going.

The King's Head Inn represents a St. John River Valley inn of about 1855. The building was originally a farmhouse, designed and constructed for a local family by carpenter James Mitchell, whose fine work is seen in several Kings Landing buildings. The King's Head is an example of Classic Revival architecture, the popular style at the time, which incorporates elements of ancient Greek design, usually as decoration. On the front of the King's Head, the corner boards, which mimic fluted columns, and the doorway, which echoes a temple entrance, are notable Classic Revival features.

A 19th century cask

Today, although the King's Head no longer offers accommodation to travellers, it is a working inn. The downstairs tap rooms provide ale to the visitor, while upstairs the dining room serves fine meals from authentic Victorian recipes.

Inns were essential and numerous in the early to middle 19th century, when travel by road — or river — was usually slow. Quality and standards varied greatly, from taverns keeping the bare minimum of "two good beds," required by law as a condition of the liquor licence, to substantial inns and hotels. A local term for inns was "half-way houses" — places to break the journey at mid-

The King's Head offers traditional meals to visitors

THE LINT HOUSE

Lawrence Lint, who with his wife Catherine and three small children occupied this house in 1830, was of Dutch descent, the son of a New York Loyalist. In both generations, the Lints were typical of many New Brunswick Loyalist families. Lawrence's father and uncle had served as privates in one of the Loyalist regiments, and in return for their service received small grants of land in Queensbury. Here they settled, and here Lawrence, one of eight children, was born around the turn of the century.

Carrying firewood was a daily year-round task in the 19th century

The Lints were hardworking but far from wealthy, and it must often have been a struggle to make the farm provide for the needs of a growing family. Still, as young men, Lawrence and his older brother Jacob acquired a nearby lot, married sisters and settled to farm.

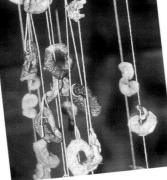

Drying for winter use

Like many small farmers, Lawrence Lint had a trade: he was a cobbler, making and repairing shoes and perhaps doing other leather work. Few village cobblers like Lint were able to make a living from their trade alone. One New Brunswick shoemaker of about this period recorded: "I sometimes make for a neighbour, and he pays me by working again for me in some other way."

The Lint House illustrates the sort of simple, industrious life that must have been characteristic of a great

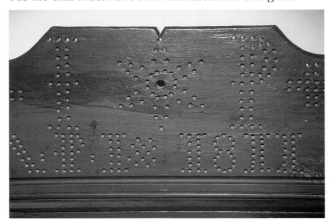

An 1811 headboard may be a re-used piece from a blanket chest

many second-generation Loyalist families. Unlike many Kings Landing homes, this one housed no servants. Catherine Lint did all the domestic work, as well as ministering to the needs of the three young children.

The house itself is a Colonial cottage, with its exposed ceiling beams and massive open fireplace. The furniture too, is simple, much of it locally made, and clearly intended for everyday use.

The open hearth with its cast iron pots

fried in a skillet. Oatmeal porridge or buckwheat griddle cakes were staples at breakfast, and often a staple at other times in poorer families.

Open fires had other characteristics and they were often smoky, and coping with the dust, wood ashes and soot they produced was a constant daily struggle. Leisure time was a scarce commodity for the women who ran the kitchens of the 19th century.

Like most of the Kings Landing houses dating from the first half of the 19th century, the Lint House has a fireplace for cooking. These open hearths were sometimes romanticized by later writers, but the day-in, day-out realities of preparing the family's meals this way must have been much less romantic. Most of the pans, skillets and pots were heavy cast iron; trivets, spits, pokers and other necessary utensils were also iron, often made by a local blacksmith. A great deal of bending, stooping and heavy lifting was required. The meals cooked here included stews of meat and vegetables, breads baked in an iron bake kettle or in a built-in bake oven, meats spit-roasted or

Exposed beams and storage cupboards in the kitchen

The Lint House traces its architectural roots through colonial styles to the old English cottage

The blacksmith shop opens its double doors wide for customers

Throughout the 19th century, almost every rural community had a resident blacksmith. At the peak of the old horse-powered economy and before railways transformed transportation in the 1870's, local blacksmiths were essential resources.

Around 1870, the period which the re-created blacksmith shop at Kings Landing displays, the vast majority of rural blacksmith shops were small, one or two man operations. The smith was a farrier, shoeing the community's horses and oxen, and also a general worker in iron and steel, making and mending tools and utensils. He might, as well, be a rough veterinarian, the horse doctor for the village.

In the final quarter of the 19th century, many blacksmith shops were in transition. Mechanization was coming in, changing both the sort of work the local blacksmith did and the way he did that work. By the 1890's, Mr. Eaton's new catalogue was arriving regularly from Toronto, offering a range of mechanical implements: not only tools for smithies, but also products to compete with their output. Some blacksmith shops expanded, growing into carriage and wagon factories while maintaining the blacksmith work as something between a sideline and a significant part of the overall business. A few shops developed into foundries; casting stoves and agricultural machinery. But most shops stayed small, slowly evolving in the 20th century to make the repairs required by automobiles and tractors. Even today, there are rural garages which can trace their origins to 19th century blacksmith shops.

What sort of work was done in a blacksmith shop of 1870? An inventory of materials from a small general shop of the period gives some insight. When Henry Lynch, a York county blacksmith, died in 1868, among his goods and chattels were 119 lbs of three different grades of steel, 833 lbs of three types of iron, 34 lbs of iron scraps, 82 horseshoes, 7 pevies, as well as links, wiffletree irons, pevie bands, horse nails, neck yokes, and the anvils, bellows, hammers, chisels, drill, punches, files and tongs necessary to his trade.

Lion and Bright, the traditionally-named Kings Landing oxen, begin their working day

The Ox Barn

One of the noticeable transitions in farming in 19th century New Brunswick was the gradual replacement of oxen by horses. For the Loyalist farmers, ox teams provided the power to do the farm work that human muscle couldn't do alone. Oxen pulled carts and ploughs, dragged harrows, even twitched logs. They were cheaper to acquire than horses, took less time to raise to working age, were hardier, much stronger and easier to feed. And, as an 1817 entry in Frederick Dibblee's diary suggests, oxen had a final edge on horses: "Everet Killed the Old Ox — Good ... — The Ice Thick this Morning for the first Time,

Except a little in Octr. Cut up and Salted Beef...."

As farms became better established and farming technology changed, oxen began to lose out. Improved breeds of horses became more readily available. They were faster than oxen, and able to pull machinery for which oxen were simply too slow, like the new mowing machines which reached New Brunswick by mid-century. Between 1860 and 1870, the number of oxen in York county declined by more than two-thirds; in the same decade, the number of horses increased by more than 40 percent. The decline continued throughout the remainder of the century. In the 20th century, the ox survives as little more than a figure of speech, and few of those who use "strong as an ox" have ever seen that strength being demonstrated.

THE LONG HOUSE

The story of the Long family and the property they owned provides an interesting sample of the changes many of the old Loyalist families went through in the 19th century. When Abraham Long Sr. landed in Saint John with the Spring Fleet in 1783, he was a 26-year-old Pennsylvania Loyalist. He was a veteran of nearly seven years of service on behalf of the King; first as an Armed

The Long House

the Loyalist era. The door faces the river, and is flanked by columns and sidelights with a large fanlight above, lighting the central hallway all day. The central hallway is typical of this architectural style in New Brunswick, as are the overhanging eaves and the vertical corner boards.

The Long House is typical of houses in the Valley in another way: it is a "sidehill" house with

Boatman, later in the New Jersey Volunteers, completing his military career with the rank of Corporal. Abraham Long was newly married, and he and his wife Ann eventually settled on land granted in the parish of Kingsclear, at what was subsequently known as Long's Creek.

Abraham and Ann had five sons, one of whom, Abraham Jr., remained on the family farm. The younger Abraham married Catherine Good in 1814, and father and son jointly ran the farm, as well as a sawmill, until Abraham Sr.'s death in 1833.

Around the time of his father's death, Abraham Jr. had a new house built, which is now at Kings Landing. It was Neo-Classical in style, with the formal front entry typical of houses built at the close of

a basement kitchen dug into the side of a small slope and accessible by a separate walk-in entrance. The Jones House and the King's Head Inn belong to this style of construction as well. They offer the practical seasonal advantages of keeping the heat from summer cooking fires out of the main house and providing a sheltered,

The dining room parlour was the best room in the house, reserved for special occasions

warm working space for the winter. On the main floor of the house is a parlour, dining room and a master bedroom with small bedrooms leading off the main rooms.

By 1845, Abraham Jr. and Catherine and five children, ranging in age from six-year-old Victoria to Barbara, aged 21, lived in the house. One can visualize here the sort of family social life Louisa Moore recalled in her

Hollyhocks bloom against the shingles

youth when "Ma and Pa always read aloud evenings from Shakespeare's plays, Burns' Poems etc. etc.... There were so many beautiful customs in the old days time when there were not any public amusements as in the present day...."

In 1860, Abraham sold the house and land to Charles W. Long Jr. of Eureka, California, although the family continued to live in the house as tenants.

What lay behind this sale to a relative who had apparently prospered in the West? Abraham died three years later, and his widow lived in the house until 1879, looked after by her daughter Barbara, who remained unmarried until soon after her mother's death. Six months after Barbara's marriage, Charles Long, still in California, deeded the house and property to her "in consideration of natural love and affection and one dollar." In these transactions may be seen the outline of a small family drama.

Barbara was the last of the Long family to occupy the house. The property remained in the hands of the descendants of the Loyalists, to whom it had been granted, for just over 100 years.

The Long House is restored to its 1845 condition, the home of a simple, hard-working family, not overly prosperous. The barn is at least as old as the house, and contains both hand-hewn timbers and timbers produced by a vertical saw, like the one in the Kings Landing sawmill. They may well have been produced by the sawmill owned by Abraham Long.

Detail on a traditional Maliseet-style porcupine quill decorated box

China cabinet in the dining room parlour

Fireplace in the dining room parlour

THE HEUSTIS HOUSE

The Heustis House, like its contemporaries the Hagerman and Ingraham Houses, is the work of noted local carpenter James Mitchell

John Hunt Heustis commissioned this house in the 1840's when he had completed his "three score years and ten." For architect and builder, Heustis chose James Mitchell, a local carpenter whose work may be seen in several Kings Landing houses of about this period. Mitchell, son of a respected Scottish cabinetmaker who had brought his family to New Brunswick in 1827, was married to Heustis's daughter.

A simple commode contains and can conceal the chamber pot, a necessary item of 19th century bedroom furniture

The new house may reflect Heustis' wish to provide for his survivors; Susannah, his second wife, was 20 years younger than he. The old house may have been getting shabby and hard to keep up. It had, after all, probably been built by Heustis' father Lewis, a New York Loyalist who had served six years in the Loyal American Regiment before bringing his wife and family to New Brunswick in the Fall Fleet of 1783. Lewis Heustis received a grant in Queensbury and moved there in 1787.

Perhaps the house reflects the desire of John or Susannah to imitate contemporary local society; not long before, the Hagermans and the Ingrahams had built new houses, much grander Neo-Classical homes, also designed and built by James Mitchell. The new Heustis House is smaller and simpler, but shows the talents of its builder. It does not keep up with general architectural trends: by this time, the Neo-Classical style in which it is built was already slightly old-fashioned and soon to be overtaken by the Country Gothic Revival.

Secretary and wallpaper in the parlour

Parlour

Many 19th century farm households kept a loom in the attic or loft; the weaver was often a resident spinster aunt, or occasionally a travelling professional weaver

Work table in the shed

Corn hangs to dry in the Heustis attic

Although John Hunt Heustis owned and lived on a farm, he had always been a man of business, with a good eye for opportunities. As a 21-year-old, he had been appointed an administrator of the estate of his grandfather, a position which had brought him nearly £200 in property and cash. Not long after, he took over the family farm from his father who moved to Saint John. His subsequent career can be followed in the records of property dealings, some apparently speculative investments, on all of which Heustis showed a profit. He was appointed parish surveyor of lumber and, on the expiry of his three-year term of office, petitioned the Crown for timber grants so that he and a group of friends and relatives could exploit a fine stand of pines he had found. In the 1830's, his riverside house "near the Nackawic" was a halfway stop for the tow-boat Mary Elija, which carried freight and passengers between Woodstock and Fredericton. In addition to these enterprises, he owned and operated a small tannery, passing it on to his son as a still viable small business on his death 30 years later.

In the Heustis House, life centred in the kitchen with its large cooking fireplace; all meals were served here. It was no doubt the warmest room in winter, and almost all the indoor work of the household's women was done here, winter and summer. The shed is a good example of the sort of catch-all room so essential to a working rural household.

John Hunt Heustis was 75 years old and infirm in 1850. His wife Susannah was assisted with the household work by 17-year-old Mary McKeen, a niece, and 16-year-old Amy Record, a servant. This was a common domestic arrangement of the time. The younger women earned their keep through their work, and learned the skills of household management. They may have been paid very little — if anything — but their own parents no longer had to provide for them. In large, poor families, one less mouth to feed could be a significant consideration.

A similar situation may be seen with the farm work. John's son Lewis — who lived and worked on his own farm — oversaw the management of his father's farm, but much of the work in 1850 was done by 15-year-old James Langy, an Irish servant.

THE COOPER SHOP

The Cooper Shop

Of all the rural craftsmen of the 19th century, the cooper has vanished most completely by the end of the 20th century. In the 19th century and earlier, coopering was a valuable, necessary and skilled trade. "Wet" coopers — barrel-makers whose products were designed and built to contain liquids — served a seven-year apprenticeship, and even "dry" and "white" coopers produced containers to high standards of quality.

The cooper was so necessary because the wooden barrel was the pre-eminent shipping and storage container of pre-industrial and early industrial society. Flour and salted meat,

Wheelbarrow

molasses and beer, butter and apples, nails, books and dozens of other products were shipped or stored in the barrels, firkins, puncheons, hogsheads and casks made by coopers. When, in 1840, W.T. Baird purchased in Saint John the initial stock in trade for the drugstore business he was starting in Woodstock, he guarded against the hazards of river shipping by having everything coopered up securely in

Buckets were one of the most common of the cooper's products

30 barrels for the trip. "The sinking of a tow boat between Fredericton and Woodstock," he noted dryly, "was not of infrequent occurrence." He paid four shillings a barrel for shipping.

By mid-century, the products of the cooper were meeting increasing competition from the products of factories. Barrel mills turned out cheaper products; box factories provided different options for storage and shipping, and other factories mass-produced containers of tin and glass. Small-scale coopers, like the one whose shop is reconstructed at Kings Landing, responded by diversifying, producing to local demand all sorts of barrels, buckets and pails, and even rough boxes. Some coopers followed an itinerant life, setting up shop in a village as long as there was work there, then moving on.

This small saltbox-style house is one of the earliest houses at Kings Landing, and the only one which did not originate in a rural community. The Fisher House once stood on Westmoreland Street in Fredericton, and takes its name from Peter Fisher who owned it — and may have lived in it briefly — late in the first decade of the 19th century. Fisher was one of the forebears of a notable 19th century New Brunswick family, and the house remained as a family rental property until the 1880's.

Peter Fisher came to New Brunswick with his Loyalist parents when he was only one year old. The family settled in Fredericton and young Peter received a good education by the standards of the time (and later married Susanna Williams, the daughter of his schoolmaster). He trained as a blacksmith, but clearly had ambitions beyond the trade he practised. By the age of 21 he was already a partner in a Fredericton blacksmithing business, became the sole owner soon after, and rapidly branched out into property development and speculation, banking and other business enterprises. He is best remembered, however, as New Brunswick's first historian, author of the *1825 Sketches of New Brunswick* containing "An Account of the First Settlement of the

Province." At his death in 1848, his obituary recorded that "notwithstanding he was generally engaged in active employments, he pursued a constant course of reading upon almost every subject and had acquired an amount of information which is very rarely attained."

Among notable Fisher descendants was his son Charles, a Fredericton lawyer who had taken over the Westmoreland Street properties before his father's death. Charles was a member of the legislature, served in several cabinets, became one

The saltbox-style Fisher House is the only Kings Landing dwelling the origins of which are urban

Shingles secured with handmade nails

Crocks, bottles and trays for use as well as display

of New Brunswick's Fathers of Confederation and the first Member of Parliament for York county, in which capacity he had the distinction of making the first speech in the new Dominion Parliament. He ended his career as a Judge of New Brunswick's Supreme Court.

In 1820, Peter Fisher rented this house to Matthias Valentine, an itinerant house carpenter who lived and worked in Fredericton for several years before moving on. While living in the small, simple Fisher House in Fredericton, Valentine did extensive repairs to the province's first Governor's Residence.

The stone fireplace was used for both cooking and heat

THE INGRAHAM HOUSE AND BARN

The Neo-Classic Ingraham House, c. 1840

Ira Ingraham, the owner of the Ingraham House, was a New Brunswick-born child of Loyalist parents. Born in 1785 at Fredericton, he was the son of Benjamin and Jerusha Ingraham. His older sister Hannah's description of the family experience in their New York home during the war and subsequently in New Brunswick is a harrowing account of the hardships of the time. Her father had joined the King's American Regiment at the outset of the war, leaving "a comfortable farm, plenty of cows and sheep," which "the rebels took... all away and sold the things, ploughs and all, and my mother was forced to pay rent for her own farm.... My father was in the army seven years.... Mother was four years without hearing of or from father whether he was

The garden door with its sidelights and fanlight matches the front door, maintaining the house's Neo-Classic symmetry

alive or dead: anyone would be hanged right up, if they were caught bringing letters. Oh! those were terrible times." In New Brunswick, which the family reached with the Fall Fleet in 1783, the conditions of their first winter were also grim. "We lived in a tent at St. Anne's until father got a house ready," Hannah recalls. "One morning when we awoke we found the snow lying deep on the ground all around us and then father came wading through it and told us the house was ready." When she followed him through the snow, she found "no floor laid, no windows, no chimney, no door, but we had a roof at least... a good fire was blazing and mother had a big loaf of bread and she boiled a kettle of water and put a good piece of butter in a pewter bowl, we toasted the bread and all sat around the bowl and ate our breakfast that morning, and mother said: 'Thank god we are no longer in dread of having shots fired through our house, this is the sweetest meal I have tasted for many a day.'"

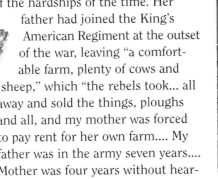

Bowl in the dining room

Gravity supplies running water in the shed

Shed

The family condition continued to improve, and Benjamin and Jerusha built up a substantial estate in Fredericton. As young men, Ira and his brother John moved from Fredericton up-river to Queensbury where they shared a farm until the 1830's, when Ira moved again, to Bear Island, where he bought land from John Heustis. Here he established a large and very prosperous farm and a number of side businesses, including a tannery and leather working shop. And here he commissioned James Mitchell to build a fine Neo-Classical style house. Ira and his wife Olive had seven children. In 1840, three adult sons and a daughter shared the house with their parents, Aunt Hannah, unmarried and by now elderly, and a cousin.

The family lived in some style and comfort, with family life presided over by Aunt Hannah, the eldest member, who lived to the age of 97, and in a sense, is said to survive to this day. In the small bedroom off the kitchen, which was used as a sickroom and where Aunt Hannah laid her healing hands on the ill, her ghostly presence is

Roses on the arbour in the Victorian garden

sometimes still felt by the sensitive. Aunt Hannah is also interesting for what she symbolizes: many of the extended families of the 19th century included unmarried women, whose presence is recorded but whose role in family life is often little appreciated. The history of the century tends in general to over-emphasize men and their roles and under-emphasize women and theirs. In reality, for the Ingrahams as for their neighbours, the family's success was quite as much due to the efforts and contributions of its female members as of its male, although the men appear disproportionately in the records.

A cosy corner in the master bedroom

One of the glories of the Ingraham House is its hedged flower garden, which blooms today with the profusion and beauty of scent and colour it must have displayed during Victoria's reign. Many of the Loyalists established flower gardens as soon as they built homes; even today, some of their descendants can point to perennials in their own gardens which originated with root divisions brought to New Brunswick by Loyalists.

Flowers had a great importance in the 19th century. In one of her

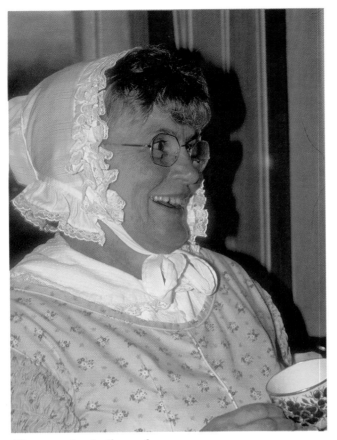

Afternoon tea in the parlour

John, where he and then his son manufactured beautifully designed and crafted furniture for more than 40 years. Nisbet pieces here include the dining table, the Regency-style sofa, games table and sofa table in the drawing room, the large mahogany desk in the upstairs office, and the huge high-post mahogany bed in the master bedroom. In the daughter's room is a Nisbet sewing stand.

The surviving work of cabinetmakers like Nisbet, and Alexander Lawrence, who made the mahogany chairs in the dining room, justifies the reputation for high quality which New Brunswick's furniture makers enjoyed in the 19th century.

The 19th century was one of the great ages of theatre. From melodrama and farce, which appealed particularly to Victorian sensibilities, to the classic tragedies of Shakespeare, the play was the thing for performers and audiences alike. In some communities, presentations were locally

Theatre at the Ingraham Barn

produced and entirely amateur. But after the railways made travel quicker and easier, there were touring companies of varying levels of ability, and their performances

letters, Louisa Moore, by then a grandmother and at least temporarily bedridden, describes her pleasure when an old friend brings her the season's first mayflowers. In another letter, she recalls that as a girl, her "pleasant task before going to church was to run to the garden, pick pinks and string them with a needle and thread so as not to lose the buds, then add southern wood sprig and rose. No one thought of going to church, or a funeral, in those days without a nosegay...."

In its interior, the Ingraham House displays another of the functions of Kings Landing: the showcasing of the work of New Brunswick's 19th century artisans. In particular, the Ingraham House shows the work of furniture maker Thomas Nisbet. Born in Scotland, Nisbet came to New Brunswick about 1813, setting up shop in Saint

A Thomas Nisbet sofa table

Secretary bookcase in the drawing room

were not always confined to the cities. For a brief period around the end of the century, the small town of Woodstock boasted "the largest theatre east of Montreal."

Kings Landing maintains the 19th century tradition of local theatre with summer performances on a stage in the Ingraham Barn.

One of the more interesting buildings in the Ingraham grouping — and one of the oldest at Kings Landing, dating from the 1790's — is the octagonal privy. Privies or outhouses were a domestic necessity in the era before indoor plumbing became commonly available, but few of them were as fancy as this. In its way, it is one of the most compelling surviving testaments to the aristocratic vision of the Loyalist elite. The privy was built for the country estate of wealthy Virginian Loyalist John Saunders, who had a distinguished military career in the Queen's Rangers before becoming Chief Justice of New Brunswick in 1822. He held this position until his death 12 years later.

The Saunders country estate consisted of some 12,000 acres, and became known as The Barony, a name which might be taken as a literal depiction of the status to which the Saunders family and their fellow members of the Loyalist elite aspired and perhaps believed they held.

The name may also have been used ironically by others, a mild mockery of the pretensions of the elite. There was a certain amount of pretence in the Saunders' Barony, though the Saunders themselves may have been slow to recognize it. Large landholdings in New Brunswick were far from being the sources of wealth and status they had been in colonial Virginia or were in England. Loyalist New Brunswick was a rural society of farmers owning and working their own land. Few wanted to rent farms from landlords. Slavery never became established — and was legally abolished at the beginning of the 19th century — and paid labour was expensive. In their dreams of large landed estates, the reach of the Loyalist elite exceeded their grasp; a state of affairs that must have been apparent to their fellow citizens. It is perhaps fitting that the Saunders' privy, which must have been recognized even in its time as an aristocrat of outhouses, survives as a reminder of The Barony.

Baking a pie in the bake oven

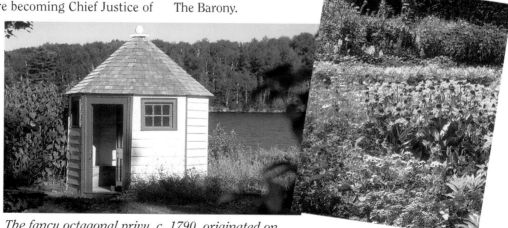

The fancy octagonal privy, c. 1790, originated on the country estate of an early Chief Justice of New Brunswick

THE MOREHOUSE HOUSE

21

Daniel Morehouse was the squire of the parish. Magistrate and Justice of the Peace, he controlled all the legal and administrative business of Queensbury parish in 1820.

Born in Connecticut in 1758, Morehouse was the sixth generation of his family to live in New England. The war interrupted his studies at Kings College (later Yale

The Georgian-style Morehouse House and its fine large barn

University); harassed by local patriot militias for his Loyalist sympathies, he travelled to New York where he enlisted in the Queen's Rangers, a Loyalist regiment. Unable to raise the money to purchase an officer's commission, he served as a sergeant. The Queen's Rangers was one of the most respected — and feared — fighting units of the Loyalist Corps, and Morehouse remained with the regiment throughout the war, rising to the rank of Quartermaster, and was mustered out with an annual halfpay pension of £40.

Morehouse and his wife Jane Gill came to New Brunswick after the war, and settled in Queensbury where the Queen's Rangers had been granted land. He received a rather large grant of 500 acres which he eventually built up to a holding of more than 1,200 acres, and began to establish a farm, a sawmill and a grist mill.

Daniel Morehouse's New Brunswick life extended beyond his involvement with his farm and mills. In 1807 and 1808, he served as Captain to a local militia company raised in response to a perceived threat of invasion from the United States, and was rewarded with an appointment as Justice of the Peace. When war clouds gathered again in 1810, Morehouse was appointed Major, commanding the Second Battalion York County Militia. He retained the post until 1818, and was known as "Major" Morehouse for the remainder of his life.

He also served in 1816 as one of the two supervisors appointed to oversee the construction of 60 miles of the "Public Road leading from Fredericton to the Canada Line." From all of his appointments he received both status and emoluments.

Public service in early Loyalist New Brunswick was expected to compensate those who performed it, and though the rewards at Morehouse's level were slight when

In hot weather, cooking in the summer kitchen avoided heating up the rest of the house

compared with those of the greater offices of government, they were a source of income in a society which was often cash poor.

His positions allowed Major Morehouse to build a new

The dining room

house in 1812. The Morehouse House is Georgian in style, in keeping with Morehouse's social standing, and characteristic of Loyalist architecture. It is two-storey, with a medium pitch roof and no eaves, and a five bay symmetrical front. Inside, the main section of the house has two large formal rooms at the front of the house with smaller rooms at the back. The staircase to the second floor is decorated in a style of trim commonly found in Connecticut.

Brass trivet in the dining room

In 1820, Daniel Morehouse and his wife Jane, both in their '60's, shared the house with an unmarried adult daughter, an adult son and his wife, and two unmarried adult sons. The elder Morehouses could be thought of as "retired" by this time, though they no doubt kept a watchful eye on the work of the younger generation. They also maintained an active social life.

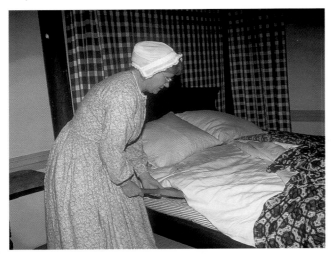

Making the beds in the 19th century included fluffing up the feather mattress

Hooking a rug in the winter kitchen

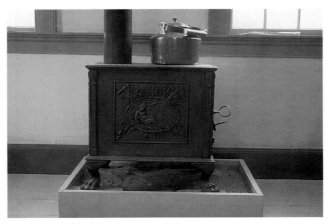

A stove in the daughter's bedroom

"Society", in the first decades of the 19th century among the Loyalist settlements of the Valley, was relatively small. "Major Morehouse" is recorded as a visitor in the journals of Reverend Frederick Dibblee who lived a day's journey upriver. In his own rural community, Dibblee often "drank tea" with his social equals ("Captn. Bull and Lady," the widow of Col. Griffith...) and exchanged evening visits. Generally, the winter was the social season, when "very good slaying" (sic) made travel easier and farming work was lighter: balls, with dancing and card playing, skating parties and other homemade entertainment enlivened the community.

In the Morehouse House, the large drawing room (the term has nothing to do with art, being derived from "with-drawing," the room one moved to after dining) was the room for entertaining. For a New Year's party, the fes-

A tall case Colonial clock, c. 1750, which belonged to Benedict Arnold during his brief residence in New Brunswick

tivities would perhaps include "hired music and an excellent supper."

Among the notable furnishings of the house is a tall case clock which once belonged to Benedict Arnold. Following the close of the Revolution, Arnold lived in New Brunswick for a time, residing briefly in both Saint John and Fredericton. He does not appear to have been a popular resident, although this impression may have been founded more on his reputation for sharp dealing in business than on the role he had played in the war. When Arnold left New Brunswick for England, he sold his household effects, the clock, a Colonial American piece of about 1750, among them.

A military relic perhaps still useful in Major Morehouse's militia career

In the Morehouse garden

THE PARISH SCHOOL

22

The establishing and improvement of schools was a continual topic of discussion in 19th century New Brunswick, although the actual improvements in public education tended to lag well behind the publicly expressed intentions.

The Parish School at Kings Landing reflects the state reached by 1840. Local village schools with some degree of public funding had begun to replace the earliest private establishments

Well-worn paths lead to the Parish School

financing was still insecure at this time), most schoolrooms were sparsely furnished and poorly equipped, and operations were often seasonal. Attendance, too, might be sporadic, governed first by the ability to pay fees, then by the competing demands of farm and household work. The availability and quality of education varied greatly from community to community.

of itinerant schoolmasters, and the schools operated under the aegis of the Church of England charity known as the Society for the Propagation of the Gospel.

Schoolmistresses were no longer a novelty by 1840, although they were still outnumbered by schoolmasters. Few teachers had received any form of training for the positions they filled.

Despite some government support (school

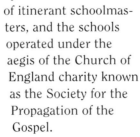

Scholars were taught largely by rote — memorization and repetition — with an emphasis on reading and penmanship. Sometimes, education was organized through the older and more accomplished students teaching the younger, a system pioneered in the Madras Schools established through the Church of England. In many rural schools, even by 1840, the Bible might be the only

Simple lessons in a sparsely-furnished school room

available book, although an 1844 inspection report for the Parish School now at Kings Landing records that the parents of the 15 scholars then attending "have supplied the pupils with Books sufficient for their present wants".

The Kings Landing Parish School is a small structure with a plastered interior and simple desks and benches. The blackboards are reproductions of 19th century homemade blackboards: made, literally, of wooden boards blackened with a mixture of shellac and stove blacking.

Later in the century, after the Common Schools Act had established a more secure basis for local education, schools began to have a more prominent social role in the community. School concerts, pie and box socials were popular events with young and old.

Education was not confined to the young. Public lectures and discussion groups for adults were common in many communities. Louisa Moore describes the "Lyceum held once a week in the Academy.... The sub-

ject for discussion has been on the merits and demerits of dancing, for two or three past weeks, which appears to be a theme brought up annually."

In summer, the Kings Landing Parish School is in session as it would have been in the summer of 1840. Today's pupils are learning about 19th century life through participating in Kings Landing's Visiting Cousins program.

THE KILLEEN CABIN

23

An immigrant's first home

Early 19th century stock barns were sometimes little more than hovels

Timothy Killeen and Mary Noonan stepped ashore in Saint John in 1822. Married at home in Ireland, the young couple had emigrated to start a new life in New Brunswick. Their arrival signalled a shift in the make-up of New Brunswick, as the Loyalist and Planter families, now in their second and third generation in the province, began to be joined by numbers of immigrants from Britain and Ireland.

There could hardly have been a greater contrast between the Ireland which Killeen and Noonan left and the New Brunswick to which they came. Ireland in the early 19th century was densely populated, a land of tiny farms: two-thirds of Irish farms were five acres or smaller. Most were farmed by tenant farmers, charged high rents

and always vulnerable to eviction by landlords. Potatoes were the staple crop, and often the only crop. In bad years, even land-owning farmers faced famine. After 1815, there were more bad years than good. Crops failed in 1816 and again in 1817. Famine and typhus stalked together through the island. Desperation bred violence: organized mobs of evicted peasants burned out new tenants and

Working outside by the cabin door on a fine day

parish. But there was no road to it, and the cost of constructing one was beyond the means of the settlers. They pooled their money to meet part of the cost, and the government eventually met the rest. The settlement was slowly established. By 1840, a provincial Emigrant Agent described it as "consisting of perhaps twenty families of hardy, industrious and meritori-

A simple hand-made pine blanket chest; the ashsplint basket on the right is probably Maliseet-made

ous natives of the Emerald Isle," adding that their land, unfortunately, was "hard and unproductive." Nor was there a local mill, and the settlers petitioned the government for a grant to build one, as it would "enable them to manufacture their own Grain, and save them from paying away their money for foreign Flour." But even with the mill, which the government approved, the farms were marginal, feeding their owners, but producing little surplus. Although they did not live on the edge of famine, the Killeen family never achieved prosperity.

Their status is reflected in their cabin. Built in 1825 of squared logs, with corners dove-tailed for strength, it is typical of the first houses raised by immigrants, and probably of the first dwellings built by most of their

attacked landlords, and, in turn, were the targets of reprisal raids. Ireland hovered on the edge of civil war. It was little wonder that many Irish chose to emigrate.

New Brunswick was a different sort of struggle altogether. Land was readily available — the government was eager for new settlers, and married immigrants qualified for grants of 200 acres. But there were conditions; the land was forested, and within five years it must be cleared at a rate of three acres for every 50 acres of the grant. As well, within three years, three cattle must be kept for every 50 acres, and a house must be built. These were not overly onerous conditions, but, as the Killeen family discovered, there were other challenges.

With a number of other families, the Killeens found land in the rear of Kingsclear

A massive stone fireplace dominates one end of the cabin

Loyalist predecessors. It is small, although two adults and two children lived there by 1830, the date the Kings Landing restoration reflects. The Killeen family included four more children by the mid-1840's, all born in the cabin. The furnishings are sparse, and most are locally made. There was little enough money for necessities, and none for luxuries.

THE GRANT STORE

24

The Grant Store re-creates the typical establishment of a late Victorian New Brunswick village general merchant.

The business was founded by Henry Colwell ("H.C.") Grant in the 1870's in Southampton. H.C.'s wife was Barbara Gartley, who before her marriage worked at Fredericton's Barker House Hotel. She is said to have been the original baker of the locally renowned Barker House Rolls, which gained much wider fame when the recipe was sold and the name changed to Parker House Rolls.

At the turn of the century, "H.C." often dozed on a chair on the porch

Around 1891, H.C. took his oldest son John Franklin ("J.F.") Grant into the business, but the two soon quar-reled, and from about 1894, J.F. ran the store alone. He also owned other local businesses — sawmills and a lime kiln — and followed the practice of paying his employees with supplies from his store. Like most general merchants of the time, he extended a certain amount of credit to most customers, and bartered farm produce for merchandise. He is remembered as developing some curious business practices in his later years, often failing to record in his ledger the name of the purchaser of an item, and later remedying the lapse by charging it to all the day's customers, arriving even-

A view of the Perley House from the Grant Store

At the village centre

tually at the identity of the actual purchaser when all the others complained!

In 1890 the Grant Store sold a wide range of yard goods, hardware and foodstuffs. It was an agent for the Connell Brothers Foundry in Woodstock, carrying its stoves and farm equipment.

An inventory of the store's stock shows some bargains by today's prices: ladies' skirts could be purchased for 85 cents; moccasins for 60 cents a pair; a cup and saucer cost six cents; beef was five cents a pound; codfish was six cents a pound. You could buy a door for $1.50 or a dung fork for a dollar.

Auctioneer

The store carried medicines and cosmetics from Allum and Balsam to Vermifuge and Worm Syrup. If all the rest failed, you could buy Panacea for 25 cents per bottle.

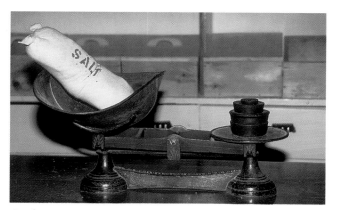

Scales

A Victorian coffee grinder

THE PERLEY HOUSE

25

The Perley House — Country Gothic Revival and Victorian decoration

The crowded parlour

Victorian "wedding china" tea service

Cast iron clock, inlaid with mother of pearl, c. 1855

Oliver Perley was a Planter, one of the colonists who moved from Massachusetts to Maugerville in the lower St. John River Valley in the 1760's. Like most of his neighbours, who numbered more than a thousand by 1776, Perley sympathized with the New England rebels. His sympathies lasted throughout the war, and in 1783 he returned to Massachusetts. Soon, however, he discovered that the reality of revolutionary democratic society was less attractive to him than the prospect had been, and he came back to live in New Brunswick.

On his return, Oliver Perley lived in Sheffield, near his former home, and apparently bought land in Queensbury, which he deeded to his son Daniel. Sometime around the end of the 18th century, Daniel and his wife Elizabeth moved to Queensbury, where they farmed, kept a tavern, and raised six sons.

The youngest son, Frederick, inherited the farm and tavern on his father's death about the middle of the 19th century. According to the family history, he built the Country Gothic Revival style house now at Kings Landing in 1866, thriftily salvaging materials from the old house to reuse in the new.

The Perley House is a Victorian gem, its Country Gothic Revival style the domestic version of the style of the church which it faces. Its exterior displays the delight in decorative detail which is typical of mid-Victorian taste.

In its interior finish and furnishings, the Perley House again epitomizes Victorian sensibilities. When it came to decoration, the Victorians, like Nature, abhorred a vacuum — any empty space should be filled, preferably over-filled. In the dining room is a pitcher commemorating the "Death of the Duke of Wellington," and in the small mahogany wall cabinet, a wedding china

Preparing a meal at the cookstove

tea service is adorned with the image of Queen Victoria, sitting regally beside her consort. Overstuffed chairs, a shadow box frame, and stuffed parrots under glass complete the picture of Victorian opulence.

Victorian social life placed great emphasis on the home. The head of many a family would have been in agreement with Louisa Moore's father when he wrote: "No society or amusements can in any way afford me happiness or contentment away from my dear family and comfortable home."

Pump organ in the parlour

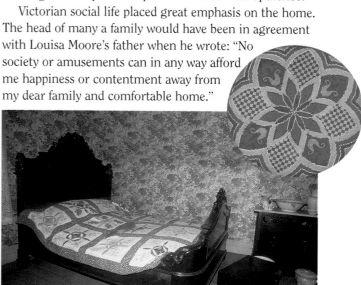

The bed in the parents' bedroom

ST. MARK'S CHURCH

26

The Loyalist settlements in New Brunswick provided for the establishment of churches. More precisely, the government provided for the "established church," the Church of England, through the reserve of church lots and glebe land to support it.

Most of the Loyalist Tory elite who controlled the government were communicants of the Church of England. Many other Loyalists, however, were not, and many more abandoned the church for the charismatic Baptist movements which swept through New Brunswick in the final decade of the 18th century and the first decades of the 19th.

In the early 19th century, Anglicanism was not in favour with the majority of New Brunswick residents. The Anglican clergy was drawn from the ranks of the elite; many of them were English gentry who had failed to secure a living at home. They were supported in their New Brunswick parishes largely through funds provided from London by the Society for the Propagation of the Gospel.

The Gothic Revival style St. Mark's, originally in Kingsclear, is one of the rural Anglican churches inspired by Bishop Medley and the building of the Cathedral in Fredericton

Many New Brunswickers adhered to the Baptist and Methodist assemblies led by lay preachers who travelled from meeting house to meeting house delivering fiery sermons and inspiring faith. They received little or no payment for their services and relied on income from farming or other work in the communities to which they ministered.

Throughout the 1820's and 1830's, Anglicanism continued to decline in influence and popularity in New Brunswick, although the Anglican clergy retained and jealously guarded their monopoly on performing marriages, a source of resentment and irritation to those following other faiths.

By mid-century,

A bride and groom at St. Mark's

Playing the organ in St. Mark's Church

Anglicanism had begun a revival in New Brunswick, spurred by the appointment of John Medley as the province's first Bishop. Medley was an enthusiastic evangelizer and a great builder of churches. St. Mark's is one of the many New Brunswick churches which can trace its origins to Bishop Medley's policy.

St. Mark's was begun in Upper Kingsclear about 1850, in part as a visible counter to the local Methodists, who had built a church there in the previous decade. The new church suffered from a lack of both parishioners and funds, remaining incomplete until 1858, when the Rector of the nearby parish of Prince William spearheaded a funding drive to finish the building.

In style, St. Mark's is Country Gothic, its steep-pitched roof an echo of the formal Gothic Revival style used by Medley in the design of Christ Church Cathedral in Fredericton. The interior furnishings of St. Mark's are made from butternut, a wood which once grew in great abundance in the St. John River Valley.

Late in the 19th century, Mr. and Mrs. John Kilburn donated to the church a triple lancet window, "made of the finest English leaded glass," in memory of their young daughter. As described in the *Daily Gleaner* of November 15, 1897, the memorial is "a triple, mullioned window [whose] centre panel is 8 feet 6 inches long and 1 foot 8 inches wide. It bears an exquisitely coloured representation of the Saviour. The side panels are each 7 feet by 20 inches in size. That on the right side beautifully represents St. John delivering his wonderful Revelation to the world, the figure of the apostle being surmounted by an eagle. The counter panel shows St. Mark, with pen and scroll, and is surmounted by a lion." The Kilburns paid $150 for the window, a significant sum at the time.

At Kings Landing, St. Mark's is a consecrated church, restored to its appearance in 1890. Regular services of the Anglican communion, including occasional marriage ceremonies, are held there.

Stained glass windows with the characteristic gothic arches

A RIVER THROUGH TIME

All rivers journey through time and space. For more than 10,000 years, after the glaciers which covered the entire land mass of New Brunswick in mile-thick ice had melted, the river we now know as the St. John has been shaping the landscape and moulding the lives of those who live in its valley.

The earliest signs of human settlement here are thousands of years old. The archaeological record is not continuous — though the human presence may have been — but thriving Native communities were well-established along the river they called Wooloostook many centuries before the first explorers from Europe "discovered" its mouth and gave it a name in their language.

Some of the Native communities of that time were inhabited seasonally, others had permanent core populations with seasonal fluctuations. There were well-used canoe and portage routes between communities and watersheds. Some villages were in part agricultural, raising corn crops on the rich alluvial intervale lands.

A timeless waterside scene

Samuel Champlain, who mapped the mouth of the river and named it at the beginning of the 17th century, was French. He called the river "Saint Jean" in honour of the saint on whose day he first saw it. Early European explorers were awed by the magnificence of the river, referring to it as "the Rhine of North America."

Throughout the century, French settlers established themselves in the land they called Acadia, settling along the coasts, increasing in numbers, living by fishing and trading, and beginning to exploit the forests and the land. They appear to have had generally amicable relations with the Native people, and used the St. John Valley principally as a safe inland travel route to and from Quebec. Their relations with the English colonists of New England were usually fractious, sometimes escalating to open and formal war when the expanding imperial ambitions of France and Britain clashed.

Early in the 18th century Acadia was formally ceded to Britain by France in the treaty which ended hostilities in 1713. Arguments as to what the boundaries of Acadia actually were continued for some time, but by mid-century the land which was to become New Brunswick was under British control. The St. John Valley, however, was still populated almost entirely by the Maliseet peoples. There were large Maliseet communities at Aukpaque — present-day Kingsclear, at Medoctec, Tobique and elsewhere. There were small Acadian communities along the river as well: at St. Anne's Point — now Fredericton — and at or near the mouths of the Oromocto and Jemseg Rivers. Acadian settlers also farmed some of the rich intervale land between St. Anne's and the Jemseg.

These Acadian communities were destroyed — and life in the Maliseet communities severely disrupted —

between 1755 and 1760. These years brought a mass forced detention of Acadians by British and New England forces, the destruction of their homes and farms in all parts of Acadia, and their forced exile in a diaspora which spread all along the coast of eastern North America, and as far away as France and the Caribbean. Some Acadians evaded capture, and many eventually made their way back to Acadia, but relatively few returned to their homes along the St. John.

Soon after Acadia had been ceded to Britain in 1713, New Englanders began to propose schemes for planting settlements in the new colony which they and the British called Nova Scotia. None of the schemes were carried out before mid-century: the risk was too great, the proponents were unable to get Royal approval, or

couldn't raise the necessary capital. With the establishment of a British fortress at Halifax by mid-century, the risk diminished. With the deportation of the Acadians it diminished still further; and with the fall of the French fortress of

Joslin Farm fields

Louisburg and the conquest of Canada, the risk vanished almost entirely. By 1760, "Planters" — a common 18th century term for colonists or settlers — from New England had begun to establish themselves in Nova Scotia, settling first on the now abandoned farms of the deported Acadians.

By 1762, the first organized Planter settlement was established in the St. John River Valley, on the rich farming land of Maugerville. Its founders had first looked further upriver, but had been warned off by the Maliseets of Aukpaque. Maugerville, and other nearby communities established later in the southern Valley, continued to draw settlers from New England and to increase in population and prosperity until the outbreak of war between Britain and its American colonies in 1775.

The Planters of the St. John River Valley took little part in the war. Some of them sympathized with the rebellious colonists, some sympathized with the Crown and the Loyal colonists. Few of them appear to have sought out the war, and the war came to them only in the form of some harassing sorties overland, and a few privateers raiding from the sea before a British fort was established at the mouth of the River in 1777–78. At the arrival of the Loyalists in 1783, there were some hundreds of Planter households in the lower Valley, concentrated in the flat alluvial intervale lands between St. Anne's and Jemseg.

The Loyalists can be accurately described as founders of New Brunswick. The province did not have an independent legal existence until after their arrival. Its creation from the northern part of Nova Scotia in 1784 was largely

Gowns of the 1840's reproduced by the Kings Landing Fabrics Department

due to the petitions of some of its new Loyalist residents who didn't want their affairs run from Halifax.

With the sudden arrival of thousands of Loyalists and the consequent major expansion of settlements, the St. John River assumed an even greater importance. Lands granted to the Loyalists began at the river. The first houses they built faced the river. It continued to be the major transportation and communication route it had been since the first Native canoe floated on its water. The Loyalists reached their new homes by boat: "We were brought as far as Maugerville in a schooner," Hannah Ingraham recalled, "[then] because the schooner could not get past the Oromocto shoals... hired a row boat from a man at Oromocto for three shillings a day...."

By the dawn of the 19th century, Loyalist settlers had spread far up the Valley. The pressure of their settlement squeezed the remaining Acadians further toward the north, and placed heavy stress on the Maliseet settlements. The Maliseets resisted the loss of their immediate village lands. When

Frontiersmen

Commissioners paddled upriver to challenge Native claims at Medoctec, they met a form of title they found impossible to invalidate. Asked for proof of ownership, the Chief pointed: "There are the graves of our grandfathers; there are the graves of our fathers; there are the graves of our children." The Commissioners retired in disarray and the Maliseets kept their land for another generation.

The river continued as the major transport route: plied by woodboats and towboats, canoes and rowboats, rafts of logs and lumber from freshet to freeze-up. In winter, its frozen surface became a "winter road marked by fir bushes planted in the ice," used by sleighs and sleds pulled by horses. In the "society" of the Loyalist elite and the British officers of the garrison, there were sleigh races on the river. Skating was a popular recreation, principally, though not only among the young.

The river showed its importance in other ways. Frederick Dibblee, the Anglican parson whose journal describes daily life in the first three decades of the 19th century, was a constant and vigilant observer of the river. He recorded the progress of the annual freshet, ever hopeful that each day's high water mark would be the season's limit. He watched the ice build from the shores and close the river each winter; he noted each run of ice and each ice jam in the spring. He set his nets at the eddy each spring and rejoiced at the "noble salmon" he caught. The river is a much stronger presence in Dibblee's journals than any of his human neighbours.

In 1816 a major change occurred on the river, in the form of the *General Smyth*, the river's first steamboat. In the decades that followed, steamboats became common on the river, although towboats continued to provide competition, particularly above Fredericton where water levels were lower.

The steamboats intensified river traffic. Manufactured and imported goods moved upstream from the port and city to the towns and villages along the river banks. The produce of the farms and forests moved downstream to supply the city, and ship overseas. Passengers moved in both directions. Each community had its wharf.

River traffic was not solely utilitarian. Summer excursions by steamboat to another community or a favourite picnic spot were popular outings. Canoeing continued to be a favourite summer pastime. In his *Seventy Years of New Brunswick Life*, Col. Baird describes a charity canoe race about mid-century when Maliseet paddlers competed to help raise money for Woodstock's Mechanics'

Institute, an early forum for adult education.

Nineteenth century progress touched more than the river. Roads were also improving, and before mid-century, a regular stagecoach service carried 15 passengers at a time on the day-long journey from Fredericton to Woodstock. As the roads were joined by railways in the final decades of the 19th century, steamboats began to decline, hurt both by the competition and, above Woodstock, by low bridges.

The changes in transportation brought other changes: the orientation of riverside communities altered. Houses were built to face the roads. Communities slowly turned their backs on the river.

River traffic continued to decline in the 20th century, and by mid-century the last steamboat had made its last run. For most of its length, river commerce consisted only of an annual drive of pulpwood. For a few days in late spring the surface of the river would be heavy with a brown mass of pulpwood, followed by crews of workers who cleared stranded pulpwood from the river banks. The

Family kin

drive was a colourful spectacle. The crews slept and ate in bunkboats and cookboats, brightly painted houseboats which drifted downstream by day and tied up along the bank in clusters at night. Bateaux and workboats crisscrossed the river transporting workers. For a few days each year the river came alive with a reminder of its earlier commercial importance.

Soon after mid-century, dams at Beechwood and at Mactaquac changed the communities along the river and the character of the river itself. The pulp drive ended. The long headponds above the dams slowed the current and deepened the river. Communities and river both took time to adjust to the changes.

In a sense, the dams, particularly that at Mactaquac, have closed a circle. The desire to preserve 19th century buildings on land which would be inundated by the headpond led to the creation of Kings Landing. And the existence of the headpond, more than 80 kilometres of deep water easily navigable by pleasure boats of all sorts from Hartland to Mactaquac, has renewed human use of the river. As well, new vistas of water and hills have provided an incentive — new houses are oriented to the river once more.

Between Kings Landing and Fredericton, visitors can cross the river on the dam to reach Mactaquac Park with its lodge, golf course, marina, beach, camping and picnic sites. Fredericton, New Brunswick's capital, has the normal amenities of a small city and is notable for its Saturday farmers' market and for the Beaverbrook Art Gallery which features a huge and imposing Dali among its holdings.

Upriver from Kings Landing, the town of Woodstock has many well-preserved large Victorian houses and the L.P. Fisher Library, an early 20th century brick building with a particularly fine interior. Upper Woodstock has a meticulously restored 1837 courthouse open to visitors. At the town of Hartland, the river is spanned by the world's longest covered bridge.

All along the river valley, the abandoned railway lines are being converted to multi-purpose trails, part of the developing Trans-Canada Trail system.

At Kings Landing one sees the St. John River spread wide, almost lake-like, as people in earlier times would have seen it only in spring freshet. Yet, at the close of the 20th century, the river continues to be the most powerful shaping presence of its valley.

RECOMMENDED READING

Bell, D.G. *Early Loyalist Saint John*. Fredericton: New Ireland Press, 1983

Condon, Ann Gorman. *The Loyalist Dream for New Brunswick*. Fredericton: New Ireland Press, 1984

Facey-Crowther, David. *The New Brunswick Militia, 1787-1867*. Fredericton: New Ireland Press, 1990

_____. *Lieutenant Colonel Joseph Gubbins, New Brunswick Journals of 1811 and 1813*. Fredericton, 1980

Finley, Gregg and Lynn Wigginton. *On Earth As It Is In Heaven*. Fredericton: Goose Lane, 1995

_____. *From The Kitchens of Kings Landing*. Fredericton, 1996

MacBeath, George, and Donald Taylor. *Steamboat Days on the St. John, 1816-1946*. St. Stephen: Print'n' Press, 1982

MacDonald, M.A. *Rebels and Royalists, The Lives and Material Culture of New Brunswick's Early English-Speaking Settlers 1758-1783*. Fredericton: New Ireland Press, 1990

MacNutt, Steward. *New Brunswick: A History, 1784-1867*. Toronto: MacMillan, 1963

Photo Credits

Legend: Top - T: Centre - C; Bottom - B; Left - L; Right - R

All photos by H.A. Eiselt except those listed below.

Photo Fredericton: p. 1; p. 2L; p. 3; p. 4TL&BL; p. 5R; p. 7R; p. 8; p. 9L; p. 10BR; p. 11; p. 12TR; p. 19 TL,BL,BR; p. 23TR; p. 29BR; p. 30; p. 51TL&BC; p. 53 TR&BR; p. 62BL; p. 65TL&TR; p. 66BR; p. 67TL; p. 68; p. 69TR.

Thanks to the following members of Photo Fredericton for their contribution to this book:

Ted Bringloe	Marg Piercey
Barb Carroll	Alfred Knappe
Don Carroll	Norma MacDonald
Barb Cowan	Roman Mureika
Janet Crawford	Ernest Rogers
H.A. Eiselt	Greg Sprague
Gladys Jeffrey	